I0177446

Love Speech

Tom Dole

Ginosko House

Flowood, MS

Love Speech

Love Speech

Tom Dole/ Ginosko House LLC
316 Northshore Pl
Brandon MS 39047
www.ginoskohouse.com

All Scripture verses are from the New King James Version of
the Holy Bible.

Love Speech. -- 1st ed.

Love Speech

Contents

Love Speech

Dedicated to Love.
And its true Source.

A Note From The Author

FROM THE GET-GO, let's make two things clear in this book:

1. God, the God of the Bible, is Love. Love is the essence of God's nature. Love is God's character. God cannot help but love, because that's who He is. The very character and nature of God is Love, and He loves _you_!

God is not fickle. It is not in His character to love you if you do good things and to not love you if you do bad things. God does not love you because you have corrected or improved your behavior. Your behavior has nothing to do with whether or not God loves you. God loves you because love is the essence of His character. It is God's character and nature to love. It does not make any difference how you behave – right or wrong, obedient or disobedient, good or evil - God loves you. God is love. He loved you then, He loves you now, and He will always love you.

2. God, the God of the Bible, is righteous. Righteousness is the essence of God's nature. Righteousness is God's character. God cannot help but be righteous, because that's who He is.

1

Love Speech

Because the very character and nature of God is righteousness, He will always do what is just and right. Because righteousness is the very essence of who He is, God hates sin. He hates sin because it keeps us separated from Him and from His love for us. The righteous character of God demands that sin be punished because it violates His standards of righteousness.

Because man is created in the image of God, He expects the same from us. To expect anything less would be to compromise His character and nature of Love and Righteousness.

Why make these two points at the start of the book? Because this book deals with issues many people consider contentious. This book will deal with the difference between 'hate speech" and "Love Speech." Many people today consider the truths found in the Bible to be "hate speech" because those truths go against their desire to pursue behaviors that, while pleasurable in the short term, are very harmful – physically, mentally, emotionally, and especially spiritually – in the long term.

What we will be discussing in this book

God loves you enough to tell you - Love Speech - the kinds of behavior that will keep you from receiving His love. The problem is not just that a particular behavior is wrong. The problem is this: if we persist in that behavior it will separate us from any fellowship with God – forever!

God's greatest predicament is two-pronged:

1) Finding a way to judge mankind's sinfulness. God must make sure that the penalty for our sins – the death penalty - is paid. This will allow Him to maintain His righteous character.

2) Finding a way to restore His relationship with a sinful mankind so He can pour out His love toward us. This will satisfy His Love character.

Mankind's greatest predicament is our innate sin nature. Our very nature is not love, nor is it righteousness. Our character and nature is one of selfishness and bad behavior. Our words, actions, and lifestyle of sin are what separate us from the Love of God. Furthermore, we are powerless in and of ourselves to stop our sinful actions and lifestyles.

So, how can God, who is both Love and Righteousness, see to it that the death penalty for our sins is paid, yet ensure that our Love relationship with Him is restored? This is a

Love Speech

predicament that only the death of God Himself can resolve!

It will be important to keep these points in mind as we discuss the problems and issues of what most people have come to call "Hate Speech."

Tom Dole

CHAPTER 1

Hate Speech

YOU HEAR A LOT ABOUT hate speech these days. Generally, hate speech is defined as "any speech that attacks, threatens, or insults a person or group on the basis of national origin, ethnicity, color, religion, gender, gender identity, sexual orientation, or disability.[1]

Does this mean every behavior should be allowable just because there is a group of people who - based on their "national origin, or ethnicity, or color, or religion, or gender, or gender identity, or sexual orientation, or disability", or whatever - enjoy that particular behavior?

No, it does not.

"Attacks, threatens, or insults". So, if

someone tells you what you are doing is wrong, and you will end up getting hurt, plus you could end up hurting other people, why is that hateful? How is that hateful? If someone is expressing a concern that you could be involving yourself in a harmful behavior, what would make you think that person hates you? Have they not just expressed a degree of concern and care for your well-being? When did it become acceptable, even commendable, to let people do whatever they want with total disregard towards the consequences?

If we truly love someone, we should be willing to risk our relationship with them by letting them know that the actions they are involved in are wrong, and that those same wrong actions are ruining the relationship. Is that really "hate speech?" If it is "hate speech" to tell someone their actions are self-destructive, then what is "Love Speech"?

Why is it considered "Love Speech" only when we affirm a person and their behavior, even though their behavior is harmful to themselves and those around them? Could "Love Speech" include warning someone about their self-destructive behaviors? Surely, we shouldn't be so naive as to allow people to pursue whatever actions they want without any consideration of the end result.

Love Speech

From the perspective of a Christian, the question could be asked as it was by Penn Jillette, a comedian, and self-professed atheist: "How much do you have to hate somebody to believe that everlasting life is possible and not tell them?"[2]

The Bible is clear that we are all going to live forever. The question is, will we live forever in heaven or in hell? So, let's re-phrase Penn Jillette's question:

If you believe a person is involved in a behavior that will not only hurt them but will prevent them from experiencing eternal life in heaven, why is it considered hate speech to warn them of the consequences they face?

According to Penn Jillette, real hate speech would be to not tell people about heaven and hell. We should at least tell them what the Bible says. The decision to pursue or not to pursue that behavior will then be up to them. Penn Jillette went on to say, that if he believed beyond a shadow of a doubt that a truck was coming at you and that you were unaware of the danger, he would tackle you, meaning that he would do all he could to get you out of danger.[3]

If Christians truly care for people, then we should be willing to risk the relationship by telling them what they are doing is wrong. But, in today's hyper-sensitive society, it's not only allowable but proper to tell someone that it is okay with us if they want to engage in harmful behavior, even though they will end up getting hurt. Especially if that is what they really want to do. Now that is the real "hate speech!"

Trying to tell someone that their words and actions are wrong is most likely when people will call out "hate speech!" The general exclamatory is along the lines of, "You're wrong to impose your values on me." Or, perhaps just the childish outcry, "You can't tell me what to do!" For some strange reason, it has become inappropriate to tell someone that their words and actions might be wrong, especially if those words and actions fall into the category of being politically incorrect. And it has increasingly become the case to be accused of "hate speech" when attempting to speak out on the moral principles stated in the Bible.

CHAPTER 2

What is "Truth"?
The Right to Be
Your Own god
(Yes, that's a small "g")[1]

'IF IT FEELS GOOD, DO IT' is a philosophical adage left over from the 1960s. However, in reality, that philosophical attitude has been around for eons. A person should be able to do whatever they think is right and makes them feel good. This is nothing other than moral relativism, and as I said, it's been around as long as there have been people. Humanists love this way of thinking (non-thinking?) It was the humanist John Dewey who said,

Love Speech

"There is no God and there is no soul. Hence, there are no needs for the props of traditional religion. With dogma and creed excluded, then **immutable truth** is also dead and buried. There is no room for fixed, natural law or **moral absolutes**." (Emphasis added.)

That's just a ten-dollar version of the ten-cent phrase, "If it feels good, do it." It is a weak attempt to provide an excuse for people to do whatever it is that makes them "feel good" without having to be concerned about the consequences of whatever it is they are doing.

The Bible describes moral relativism this way: *"Every man did what was right in his own eyes."*[2] That is moral relativism in a nutshell. Here are a couple of other things the Bible has to say about moral relativism:

Woe to those who are wise
in their own eyes,
and prudent in their own sight![3]

There is a generation that is pure
in its own eyes,
yet is not washed from its filthiness.[4]

The way of a fool is right in his own eyes,
but he who heeds counsel is wise.[5]

Love Speech

In light of what the Bible says, John Dewey's statement, along with the old 60's cry of libertines, "If it feels good, do it," and all sentiments like them, are entirely self-serving and self-deceiving. They are statements made in an attempt to explain away personal responsibility with the desperate hope of being able to pursue whatever makes a person feel good, regardless of whether that feeling is right or wrong. We should never underestimate man's ability to rationalize away his responsibility for his words and actions.

In the world of moral relativism, there are – supposedly - no absolute truths. Of course, we should all have the understanding that this argument has no logic base on which to stand. In making the statement 'There are no absolute truths' we would be stating an absolute truth. This makes the statement false. Therefore, there are absolute truths. It is an unchanging truth that there are absolute truths.

Nonetheless, for those who espouse moral relativism, it is okay for a person to have a set of "truth-values" that will fit their situations and lifestyles, while at the same time allowing another person to have an entirely different set of truth-values, even though they are for the same situations and lifestyles. Just don't try to impose your truth-values on someone else!

Love Speech

That is what moral relativists consider "hate speech."

You have your "truth", they have their "truth". What's "good" for you may not be "good" for them. What is true in one area of your life, perhaps your social life, doesn't need to be true in another area of your life, say your business life. All morals become relative in any given situation. "You can't tell me what to do!", cries the child, "That's hate speech!"

This free-wheeling view of "truth" allows a person to perform a broad range of moral gymnastics. It allows a person multiple methods of easing the pain of a guilty conscious. As was previously stated, never underestimate a man's ability to rationalize away his personal responsibility for his words and actions.

But the issue still remains. There are absolute truths. There are no square circles, and there are no round squares. So, the question becomes, what are the absolute truths we should be living by?

CHAPTER 3

Truth or Dare!
Absolutes vs. Relativism

"WHAT IS TRUTH?" JESUS ANSWERED THAT QUESTION with a plain and straightforward statement: *"God's Word is Truth."*[1]

Absolute truths are dependable and applicable at all times, in all places, and for all people. They do not change with social standards. Absolute truths do not change with men's thinking and customs, nor with men's laws. There is no law that can be legislated or adjudicated that alters or dissolves an absolute truth. If it was truth when it was first recorded, it is still truth now. If it was truth for one generation, it is still truth for this generation, and it will remain truth for all future generations.

When it comes to absolute moral truth, God says what He means and means what He says. And, it makes no difference what the situation or circumstances are, He doesn't change His mind.

In order to be stable and effectual, any individual, family, or government must be grounded in a moral law system. But, the kind of thinking that leads to moral relativism – every man doing what is right in his own eyes - tends to destabilize people, families, and nations.

Why?

Under moral relativism truth changes from moment to moment, day to day, from situation to situation. Under moral relativism, all foundations are shifting sand. What pressure group has the most influence today? That group will determine what today's "truth" is until it is replaced by a new pressure group. Or, until the situation changes and "truth" must be redefined so that the current pressure group can maintain its power. Biblical morality is grounded in the immutability of God's laws and God's Word, not man's law or man's word. And certainly not in what pressure group currently holds sway. God's Word does not change. It endures and can be applied in the same manner from situation to situation, from generation to generation.

So, it turns out that John Dewey was completely wrong. His statement must be rephrased:

"There is a God, and all men have a soul. All men will be required to give an account of how they used the life God gave them. Hence, there is a great need for the props (sic) of traditional Christianity. The dogma and creed of Christianity are immutable. The truth of God's Word endures from generation to generation. Fixed, natural law is a must. Moral absolutes are a necessity for soundness and stability in the life of an individual, a family, and a nation."

The problem in today's society is that most statements dealing with absolute truth, such as those found in the Bible, are denounced as "hate speech". "You can't tell me what to do!" The challenge for true Christians becomes this: will we stand on the Truth, or will we try to build on a foundation that shifts from day to day, from situation to situation? Which foundation will you dare to build your life on?

Love Speech

CHAPTER 4

Love & Relationship vs. Truth

ONE OF THE PRIMARY EXAMPLES of moral relativism is found in the thinking that relationships must be preserved at all costs and at whatever expense, even at the expense of your position regarding truth. In order to hold on to and maintain a relationship, you must be willing to give up your defense of a truth. You cannot point out a person's wrong behavior as stated in the Bible, because in doing so you might ruin the relationship. You can believe whatever you want, just don't believe it too strongly, especially if it could cause the demise of a relationship. This manner of thinking makes people relationally strong but ethically and intellectually lazy.[1]

The real issue is this: relationships must be based on truth. If people in a relationship agree on what truth is, the relationship will be strong. If people in a relationship do not agree on what truth is, the relationship will be weak at best, or non-existent at worst. If truth is constantly being manipulated then there is no foundation for the relationship to stand on. Once the truth - yours or theirs - changes, the relationship begins to crumble and ultimately dissolves away. Such is the case so often today in personal, family, business, political, and even national relationships. Once the dispute over truth begins, accusations of hate speech are hurled. Hate speech because "you" are disagreeing with "me" over what my view of truth is.

Sacrificing your view of a moral truth in order to keep a relationship is what some people call "loving your neighbor as yourself." This, however, is not the way Jesus defined "loving your neighbor" in the Bible. Moral relativists say people should be free to do what makes them happy. (Side Note: This is *not* what the phrase "pursuit of happiness" means in the U.S. Constitution). As long as they are not bothering people, they should be free to do what they want to do. "If it feels good, do it." One more time: This is not how Jesus defines *"love your neighbor as yourself"* in the Bible.

Love Speech

The bottom line is, that in order to preserve any relationship, that relationship must be built on a foundation of truth, and that truth must be unchanging and absolute. The only thing that will allow a relationship, or a life, to endure, persevere, and thrive in a world of lies, deceit, and deception, is absolute truth. So, what did Jesus mean when He said, *"You shall love your neighbor as yourself?"* We'll get to that in a couple of chapters.

Love Speech

• CHAPTER 5 •

Biblical Love Speech

"FOR YOUR OWN SAFETY…"

Real Love Speech always has the other person's best interests in mind. If we truly love and respect people shouldn't we at least try to find a way to tell them truths which may help them avoid problems and provide long-term benefits in their lives?

The correct answer to that question would be, "Yes!"

The first thing people need to know is this: *God Is Not Mad At You!* Most people should be very familiar with John 3:16 *"For God so loved the world that He gave His only begotten Son…"* But, if you tell somebody that God loves them, they usually respond by saying they have done too many bad things in their life for God to love them, let alone for God to see any value in them and even want to save them. Far too many people believe God is mad at them. What people are not so familiar with is the verse that comes right after John 3:16,

"God did not send His Son into the world to condemn the world..."

God is not mad at people. He is not mad at you, or me, or anyone else. The Bible says, *"God is Love."*[1] Notice that this is a complete sentence! There is a period at the end of it. "God is Love." Period. End of report. God is Love. God made you. God made you for the precise purpose of showing you how much He loves you. Therefore, you are made for God's love. You are not made for failure, fear, poverty, illness, death, or any other nasty stuff. You were made to be a recipient of God's Love.

However, the Bible also says God is holy. What God is mad at is sin.[2] Why does God hate sin? Because sin goes against His very nature, and sin is what separates people from Him and from His love.

"Your sins have separated you from your God..."[3]

Sin keeps you in failure, fear, poverty, illness, death, and all that other nasty stuff. Sin keeps you from getting to know and experience God personally. God is love. He created you to be a recipient of His love. But sin keeps you from the love God has for you. God hates the behaviors and lifestyles that separate us from Him. Lifestyles that involve sin keep you from experiencing God's best. His success, not failure. His love, not fear. His riches, not poverty. His health, not illness. His life, not death. His joy, not depression. His good things, not bad things.

The God of the Bible is a God of relationship. He desires a personal relationship with you and He said so: *"This is eternal life, that they may <u>know You</u>* - by personal experience - *the only true God, and Jesus Christ whom You have sent."*[4] God loves you! He hates anything that comes between you and Him. He hates anything that spoils your relationship with Him.

God's highest desire is for you to know Him – personally! So, in His Word, God tells you what types of wrong behavior will keep you from knowing Him. These are absolute truths. These behaviors will *always* separate you from God. God tells you what will cause fear and keep you from His love. God tells you what will cause disease and keep you from His health. God tells you what will cause failure and keep you from His success. God tells you what will cause depression, poverty, and bad things and keep you from His joy, riches, and good things.

God loves you so much that He will openly tell you what things you should not do. Why? Because those things will hurt you, they will hurt the people you love, and they will prevent you from having the relationship with Him that He desires you to have.

God loves you. God does not condemn people who are involved in these behaviors and lifestyles. Yet, neither does God condone or confirm these behaviors and lifestyles just because He loves you. God loves you enough to warn you that if you continue to persist in these lifestyles and behaviors, they will ultimately separate you from Him for all eternity! God loves you enough to say, "For the sake of your own safety, don't do these things." God loves you enough to say, "For your benefit, do this instead." This is called "Love Speech."

The problem is, people see God as someone trying to keep them from doing what makes them "feel good". So, they cry out, "Hate Speech!" Love Speech is the opposite of hate speech. Hate speech is all about me, me, me, and mine. "Don't tell *me* what to do."

Love Speech

"Don't try to impose your values on *me*." "You can't tell *me* what's right and wrong!" No, I can't. But God can. And He does just that in the Bible. I'm just reiterating what God has already said. Love Speech will uphold the absolute truths of God's Word. Love Speech points out what the absolute truth is, and the corrections that need to be made to line up with that truth. Love Speech points out the dangers of not making those corrections and the benefits of following God's truth. God's Love Speech has your best interests in mind.

Hopefully, the light is beginning to dawn that not everything that makes you "feel good" is actually good for you. Hopefully, you're beginning to understand that when you hear the warning to stop immoral behavior, it's not hate speech. It's Love Speech!

People who believe that truth and morals are relative to any situation still teach their children not to play with an electrical outlet. Why? The children are having so much fun, they are exploring and learning. The children should be free to be uninhibited, free to express themselves, free to be who they were born to be. Why would they tell their children to quit playing with the electrical outlet?

Love Speech

Because they know there's an absolute truth involved: it's either their children or the electrical outlet! They love their children. They don't want their children to have anything bad happen to them. You know, like getting electrocuted. They may flip-flop on other issues, but not on that one! God is the same way. He doesn't want anything bad to happen to you. So, He warns you, "Don't do that! You'll get hurt!" Love Speech is telling someone they are about to violate an absolute truth which will cause unwanted problems in their lives and in the lives of others around them. "For your own safety, don't stick your finger in the electrical outlet. You'll get hurt!"

•   CHAPTER 6   •

How To Hate
Your Neighbor

WHAT DO WE REALLY MEAN when we say to someone, "I love you?" Real love is a commitment that goes far beyond physical and emotional desires. So, when we say, "I love you", just how much of a commitment are we making? Are we committed to "love" only until we get what we want physically? Are we committed to "love" as only as long as the other person keeps feeding our emotional desires? Once the physical need is met, or the emotional desires are no longer met, is love over and done with?

Most of us are all familiar with different categories of love: erotic, friendship, brotherly, and unconditional. Much has been written on these various topics of love, and this is not an attempt to add to those volumes (and there are volumes!) What we will do is take a look at the commitment involved in love, specifically from a Biblical point of view.

We mentioned before that when Jesus talked about "loving your neighbor as yourself", He wasn't talking about letting your neighbor do whatever makes them "feel good." He wasn't talking about going along to get along. What He said was this: *"Love your neighbor **as yourself**."* If you know you shouldn't stick your finger in the electrical outlet because you could get hurt, then you should also warn your neighbor about sticking their finger in the electrical outlet. Most people, Christian or not, moral or not, tend to think this is a good principle to live by. But, let's take a much closer look at this truth. When Jesus said, *"Love your neighbor as yourself,* here's the Scripture He was referring to:

> *"You shall not*
> *hate your brother in your heart.*
> *You shall surely rebuke your neighbor,*
> *and not bear sin because of him.*
> *You shall not take vengeance, nor bear any*
> *grudge against the children of your people, but*
> *you shall love your neighbor as yourself:*
> *I am the LORD."*[1]

Love Speech

Usually, the only element we hear about this Scripture verse is, *"Love your neighbor as yourself."* However, the added information puts this practice of "loving your neighbor as yourself" in an entirely different light.

"You shall not hate your neighbor in your heart."

To stand by and watch someone engage in a behavior or lifestyle that will prove to be self-destructive, and will end in fear, failure, and loss, ultimately cutting off their relationship with God for all eternity, is a type of hate speech. To allow someone to engage in a harmful behavior just because it makes them "feel good" is to *hate your neighbor in your heart*. Hate speech is to *not* warn someone that they are involved in a behavior that will ultimately hurt them. Remember Penn Jillette. He would tackle you if he knew you were about to be run over by a truck. (But playing in the street is so much fun!)

"You shall surely rebuke your neighbor and not put up with sin because of him."

A "rebuke" should be in the form of Love Speech, a loving warning, with the idea in mind of helping them re-think their desires and the consequences of their actions. If your neighbor is involved in a sinful behavior, you are not to put up with that sin without talking to your neighbor about it. That would be hate speech.

> *"You shall not take vengeance,*
> *nor bear any grudge*
> *against the children of your people"*

Our words are not to be in the form of an "attack, threat, or insult." The idea is to warn and help, not attack and condemn. Remember John 3:17, *God did not send His Son into the world to condemn the world, but that the world through Him might be saved.* You can't save someone when you're just standing idly by without saying anything. Love Speech is required. However, once the warning has been given, you cannot "take vengeance" against your neighbor if they decide to continue pursuing their errant course.

> *"You shall love your neighbor*
> *as yourself."*

If we were about to engage in a behavior that will bring hurt and shame into our lives, we would surely want someone to warn us and try to save us from that behavior. We are to be just as thoughtful and considerate of our neighbors.

With this perspective in view, the real hate speech is telling your neighbor, "Well, if you want to do that because it makes you feel good, that's okay. It is wrong according to the Bible, but if you want to do it, then it's no concern of mine and it's okay with me." That is hate speech defined! What you are really saying is, 'Do whatever makes you feel good, even though it will hurt you." That is *not* loving your neighbor, that is the hate speech of moral relativism!

Moral relativists do not have their neighbor's best interests at heart. They are allowing their neighbor to play with "electrical outlets", even though they know such conduct will hurt them. When moral relativists do that, the Bible calls it *"hating your brother in your heart*!" You are "*putting up with sin because of him*." Failure to warn a person of the consequences of sinful activities is hate speech!

So, if we are truly going to practice Love Speech, and not hate speech, we will tell our neighbors when they are doing something wrong according to the absolute moral truth of the Bible. Don't stick your finger in the electrical outlet! You'll get hurt!

One more time, notice the context of how we are to "love our neighbor". It is in the context of Love Speech. If our neighbor is engaged in an activity or lifestyle that goes against the absolute truth of biblical doctrine, we are required to point out the problem to them. Ouch! This can be difficult. Especially when you can be accused of hate speech.

Far too many churches allow this type of "hate speech". They do not truly "*love their neighbor as themselves*." If they did, then instead of telling them sin is okay, they would declare the truth to that person, even at the risk of losing the relationship. Yet, with the hope of helping that person realize their error, correct their lifestyle, and grow closer to God.

CHAPTER 7

Examples of
Real Love Speech

BEFORE WE LOOK AT SOME EXAMPLES of Love Speech found in the Bible, there are a few things we really should remember:

1. Remember John 3:17. God is not mad at you. God loves you. God did not send Jesus to condemn people. He sent Him to save people.

2. God does not want His children playing around "electrical outlets." God hates sin – things that hurt people, things that cause people to have poor relationships, get sick, and so forth. God hates those behaviors and lifestyles that keep people separated from Him.

3. God wants his best for you: His love, not fear. His health, not disease. His success, not a failure. His joy, not depression. His riches, not poverty. His good things, not bad things.

As noted in the Lev. 19:17-18, part of Love Speech includes pointing out the wrong activities a person is taking part in: *You shall not hate your brother in your heart. You shall surely rebuke your neighbor, and not bear sin because of him.*

Love Speech has two parts. First, pointing out the person's erroneous words and actions. Not for the purpose of ridiculing or debasing the person, but simply for making them aware that they are engaged in words and actions that will cause harm. There should be some care and concern shown. Also, remember that we are not to *"take vengeance or hold a grudge because of his sin."* This means we are not to ridicule, threaten, or insult those who decide to continue in their harmful behaviors and lifestyles. However, we are responsible for pointing out what the wrong behavior is and what its consequences are.

The second part of Love Speech is showing your neighbor what changes in thinking and action are required to open the way for God's benefits to come into their lives.

Love Speech

Remember: God is love. God loves people. God hates sin. God doesn't want the people He created to get hurt or have anything bad happen to them. He certainly doesn't want them to die. Most certainly God does not want people to be involved in things that keep them separated from Him and his love for them. So, He warns them of activities they should not be involved in. Then He provides the means of leaving those activities and lifestyles behind and living the life He intended them to live. With these thoughts in mind, here are some examples of God's Love Speech.

1. *You shall have no other gods before Me.*[1]

Did you know that the God of the Bible is the only one who declares His love for you? All other gods merely tell you what you must do in an attempt to gain their favor or approval. None of the other gods loved you enough to die for you. In fact, many of the other gods want you to die for them!

2. *You shall not make for yourself a carved image —*
any likeness of anything
that is in heaven above,
or that is in the earth beneath,
or that is in the water under the earth;

Love Speech

you shall not bow down to them
nor serve them.[2]

The problem with idols is this: we become like the gods we worship.[3] So if you worship idols of stone that are cold, unresponsive, and impersonal, you will become cold, unresponsive, and impersonal. Is the world materialistic, harsh and unforgiving? If you worship the world, you too will become materialistic, harsh, and unforgiving. If you worship Christ, you will ultimately become like Him - Love. That is Love Speech!

3. You shall not take the name of the LORD
your God in vain,
for the LORD will not hold him guiltless
who takes His name in vain.[4]

This has little to do with language and everything to do with accurately representing Christ - LOVE - before an unbelieving world.

4. Remember the Sabbath day,
to keep it holy.[5]

God desires fellowship with His people. So, He set aside one day each week for that purpose.

5. Honor your father and your mother,
that your days may be long upon the land
which the LORD your God is giving you.[6]

Love Speech

6. You shall not murder.[7]

7. You shall not commit adultery.[8]

8. You shall not steal.[9]

*9. You shall not bear false witness
against your neighbor.*[10]

*10. You shall not covet your neighbor's house;
you shall not covet your neighbor's wife, nor
his male servant, nor his female servant, nor
his ox, nor his donkey, nor anything that is
your neighbor's.*[11]

Wait just a second here! Aren't these the Ten Commandments? Why yes, they are! Isn't it amazing the lengths society takes today to avoid having even the chance of hearing God's Love Speech? Why is this Love Speech and not hate speech? Because disobedience in these areas is like sticking your finger in an electrical outlet. It's harmful! These are behaviors that keep you from experiencing the Love of God: His success, His riches, His health, His life, His joy, His good promises.

When God's Love Speech should be posted on all four corners of every intersection in the country, society attempts to make it against the law to post them nearly anywhere.

Love Speech

But take heed!

The words of the wise are like goads,
and the words of scholars
are like well-driven nails...
and further, my son, be admonished by these.[12]

What follows are a few more examples of God's Love Speech for some of society's hot-button issues today. For your own benefit, don't poke your finger into any of these "electrical outlets!"

Love Speech for Homosexuals

Leviticus 18:22
You shall not lie with a male as with a woman.
It is an abomination.

Romans 1:26-27
"For this reason (not recognizing God as Creator of all things) *God gave them up to vile passions. For even their women exchanged the natural use for what is against nature. Likewise also the men, leaving the natural use of the woman, burned in their lust for one another, men with men committing what is shameful, and receiving in themselves the penalty of their error which was due."*
(See also: Lev. 18:22-24; Lev. 20:13; and
1 Cor. 6:9-10)

Love Speech

Notice that they made these choices of their own free will. While homosexuality is not genetically ordained, it is part of the sin nature found in all mankind. Also, notice that homosexuality is *shameful* and that there is a *penalty* they receive for *their error*. John Dewey was wrong! There is a penalty for playing with an "electrical outlet." All God is saying here is this: 'For your own safety, please, don't play with the "electrical outlet" of homosexuality!'

When we know a person is involved in a wrong lifestyle, if we simply avoid telling them the truth for the sake of keeping the relationship, as mentioned previously, we are "*hating our brother in our heart.*" We know this person is involved in a destructive lifestyle. But just so we can keep the relationship going, just so we can avoid rocking the boat, we tell ourselves that it is their decision to make, and as long as they are happy with that lifestyle it is okay. Remember Penn Jillette's question: *"How much do you have to hate somebody to believe that everlasting life is possible and not tell them?"* When we disregard an absolute moral truth for the purpose of keeping a relationship, then we have not expressed real love, we have, in fact, expressed hate speech! We have shown that we do not love that person enough to tell them of the consequence of their wrong actions.

Love Speech for Atheists

Psalm 14:1
*"The fool has said in his heart,
'There is no God'."*

A god that is small enough for your mind is not big enough to be worshipped!

Psalm 10:4
*The wicked in his proud countenance
does not seek God;
God is in none of his thoughts.*

1 Corinthians 2:14-15
*But the natural man does not receive
the things of the Spirit of God,
for they are foolishness to him;
nor can he know them,
because they are spiritually discerned.*

To a natural person, the wisdom of the Bible does not appear to be understandable because it must be spiritually discerned. Instead of denying this wisdom, a wise man would ask for God's help in understanding it. Only a fool would try to deny on an intellectual basis the reality of God and the love God has for him. An intellectual decision of choosing

Love Speech

to ignore God is like playing with an electrical outlet. This is God saying, 'For your own sake, please, don't play with the electrical outlet of not believing that I created you, love you, and have your best interest at heart!'

Love Speech for Leaders of Nations

Psalm 2:10-12
Now therefore, be wise, O kings;
Be instructed, you judges of the earth.
Serve the LORD with fear,
and rejoice with trembling.
Kiss the Son, lest He be angry,
and you perish in the way,
when His wrath is kindled but a little.
Blessed are all those
who put their trust in Him.

Love Speech for Abortion

Leviticus 20:1-5
Then the LORD spoke to Moses, saying,
"Again, you shall say to the children of Israel:
'Whoever of the children of Israel, or of the
strangers who dwell in Israel, who gives any
of his descendants to Molech (burning children alive),
he shall surely be put to death.
The people of the land shall
stone him with stones.

Love Speech

I will set My face against that man,
and will cut him off from his people, because
he has given some of his descendants to
Molech, to defile My sanctuary and profane
My holy name. And if the people of the land
should in any way hide their eyes from the
man, when he gives some of his descendants
to Molech, and they do not kill him, then I will
set My face against that man and against his
family; and I will cut him off from his people,
and all who prostitute themselves with him to
commit harlotry with Molech.

Yes. This is a tough Old Testament stance.
No. This is not an argument for those who
perform or have an abortion to be put to death.
However, God is serious about not killing
children inside or outside the womb! Why?
Because children are innocent! Notice this
next verse:

Proverbs 6:16-17
These six things the LORD hates,
Yes, seven are an abomination to Him...
hands that shed innocent blood.

Psalm 139:13-14
You formed my inward parts;
You covered me in my
mother's womb. I will praise You,

Love Speech

for I am fearfully and wonderfully made;
marvelous are Your works,
and that my soul knows very well.

Love Speech for Sexual Immorality and Pornography

Just for the record:

1. Fornication is any type of sex outside of marriage.

2. Adultery is sex with a person other than your spouse.

3. Pornography: It is not okay, all right, or acceptable to watch pornography even though you are not physically involved in the act.

Leviticus 18:6-23

None of you shall approach anyone who is
near of kin to him, to uncover his nakedness:
I am the LORD.
The nakedness of your father or the nakedness
of your mother you shall not uncover.
She is your mother;
you shall not uncover her nakedness.
The nakedness of your father's wife
you shall not uncover;
it is your father's nakedness.

The nakedness of your sister,
the daughter of your father,

Love Speech

or the daughter of your mother,
whether born at home or elsewhere,
their nakedness you shall not uncover.

The nakedness of your son's daughter
or your daughter's daughter,
their nakedness you shall not uncover;
for theirs is your own nakedness.

The nakedness of your father's wife's
daughter, begotten by your father
— she is your sister —
you shall not uncover her nakedness.

You shall not uncover the nakedness of your
father's sister;
she is near of kin to your father.
You shall not uncover the nakedness of your
mother's sister,
for she is near of kin to your mother.

You shall not uncover the nakedness of your
father's brother.
You shall not approach his wife;
she is your aunt.
You shall not uncover the nakedness of your
daughter-in-law
— she is your son's wife —
you shall not uncover her nakedness.

You shall not uncover the nakedness of your
brother's wife;

Love Speech

it is your brother's nakedness.

You shall not uncover the nakedness of a woman and her daughter, nor shall you take her son's daughter or her daughter's daughter, to uncover her nakedness.
They are near of kin to her.
It is wickedness.
Nor shall you take a woman as a rival to her sister, to uncover her nakedness while the other is alive.

Also you shall not approach a woman to uncover her nakedness as long as she is in her customary impurity.

Moreover you shall not lie carnally with your neighbor's wife,
to defile yourself with her.

1 Corinthians 6:18-20
Flee sexual immorality.
Every sin that a man does
is outside the body,
but he who commits sexual immorality
sins against his own body.
Or do you not know that your body is the temple of the Holy Spirit who is in you,
whom you have from God,
and you are not your own?

Love Speech

Acts 15:20
But that we write unto them, that they abstain from pollutions of idols, and from fornication.

Love Speech for Bestiality

Leviticus 18:22-23
Nor shall you mate with any animal,
to defile yourself with it.
Nor shall any woman stand before an animal
to mate with it.
It is perversion.

Love Speech for Transgenderism

Genesis 1:27
So God created man in His own image; in the image of God He created him;
male and female He created them.

According to the Bible, gender is binary only. The only two genders recognized by God are male and female.

Deuteronomy 22:5
A woman shall not wear anything that pertains to a man, nor shall a man put on a woman's garment, for all who do so are an abomination to the LORD your God.

Love Speech

1 Corinthians 11:14
*Does not even nature itself teach you that if a man has long hair,
it is a dishonor to him?*

1 Corinthians 6:19
*Or do you not know that your body is the temple of the Holy Spirit who is in you,
whom you have from God,
and you are not your own?*

These are but a few of the warnings to avoid the behaviors which go against the absolute truth of Biblical morality. Yet these behaviors are found everywhere in societies today. Why such severe warnings? Because the situation is serious!

All mankind finds itself in a predicament that is quite dangerous. The consequences of failing to heed these warnings are extreme. It is very much like the dire consequences of playing with an electrical outlet. In fact, the consequences are far worse. Continuing to practice these harmful behaviors and lifestyles will ultimately separate you from God and His Love, for all eternity.

Yet even with the warnings comes the outpouring of God's Love. God still loves you even if you have engaged and participated in any of these activities and lifestyles. Or in any other wrongful activities outlined in God's Love Speech. But He will not condone your continued practice of these lifestyles and behaviors. He doesn't mention the things listed above because He wants to condemn you. He mentions them so you can see the need to restore your Love relationship with Him. He stands ready to forgive you, to clean you up, to heal you, and to restore your relationship with Him.

Have you ever noticed that the "great leaders" of the Bible were *all* flawed? None of them had the character or qualities God was looking for. They were greedy, selfish, lustful, murderous, and so forth. Mankind's sinful nature was at work in all of them. Even after God became involved in their lives! The primary reason the sinful human nature of those people is explicitly told in the Bible is to show that in spite of their flaws, shortcomings, and failures, *God still loved them!*

God doesn't sugar-coat the stories in His Love Speech. But in order for their relationship with God to be restored, He still had to clean them up and deal with the consequences of their sins. He makes it clear that His love for us is not dependent on our behavior or responses to Him. He loves us whether we love Him… or not. And with His great Love, He stands ready to heal us, clean us up, and restore our relationship with Him… if we will let Him.

Love Speech

CHAPTER 8

If It Feels Good, Do It

ACCORDING TO THE PHILOSOPHIES of materialism and moral relativism so common in the worldview of today's society, the evil that men do is caused by outside forces exerting unwanted pressures on mankind. Men's faults, they say, are caused, not by what is within a man, but by pressures and forces exerted on him by outside causes. These outside forces, they say, could include his environment, his heredity, his education - or lack thereof, or any other excuses they can come up with, as long as the primary cause is outward not inward. This is in line with John Dewey's false claim that there are no moral absolutes, therefore a man can do *whatever is right in his own eyes.*" It is all a blatant attempt to avoid personal responsibility.

Love Speech

Let's face it, all mankind has a natural inclination towards wrong behavior of one type or another. Immoral behavior "feels good." If it didn't, we wouldn't do it. We all want to do what makes us feel good whether it is right or wrong. Yet at the same time, we don't want to be responsible and have to pay the consequences for our bad actions.

Have you ever noticed that you don't have to teach a child to be bad? It's just in their nature. What you really have to do is teach them good behavior and good manners.

A study was performed in 1999 by Universite de Montreal psychologist Richard Tremblay on children under the age of 18 months. The following statistics are based on observations of the 511 children in the study:

- 21% physically attack others
- 70% grab things away from others
- 46% push
- 23% fight
- 24% kick
- 27% bite

The astonishing thing was that 100% of the children in this study were engaged in one or more of these wrong behaviors. Who taught children to behave badly?

Love Speech

No one. It's in their nature to behave badly.

When did these children acquire these selfish and inappropriate behaviors? They were born with them. They acquired these behaviors long before any outside forces – education, environment, etc. – could have caused them. In short, this sounds exactly the way many adults are acting in the streets of America and around the world.

Why is this the case? Let's face it, folks, we are born to be mean. The children in the study - and adults on the streets - were born with those bad behaviors already embedded in their nature. The only effect outside forces have on the behavior of adults who act as the toddlers do, is to amplify the desire to participate in those bad behaviors. Outside forces are not the cause of the problems. Outside forces merely exacerbate the already existing internal immoral nature found in all mankind.

As a result of his study, Dr. Tremblay concluded that the real job of parents is not to teach children to be themselves. The real job of parents is to teach their children to obey moral principles. In other words, the real job of parents is Love Speech. "Don't play with

the electrical outlet. You will get hurt!"
Judging by the way adults act in public these
days - let alone children - parents really need to
start stepping up to the plate.

Human desire is warped. We are taught
from an early age that all people are basically
good, but we just make mistakes from time to
time. Actually, it is the other way around. We
are all basically wicked and we just happen to
do good things from time-to-time. A man is not
a car thief because he steals a car. A man steals
a car because he is a car thief. It's in his nature.
The problem is internal, not external. All
humans are born with the innate nature to be
wicked. Oh, most of us can cover it up to some
degree. But in one form or another something
happens each day which gives us the
opportunity, big or small, to think, talk, or act
in a wrong way. So, we do.

Therefore, we all find ourselves in a dire
predicament. It is our human nature to do
wickedness. It's impossible for us to get along
with each other. And we are incapable of
curing our nature or solving the problem by
ourselves - no matter how many laws we pass.
If it is not the outside forces of a man's
environment, then what does cause the
problem of wicked and immoral behavior in
mankind? A Biblical worldview offers the only

sound and reasonable answer.

Sin.

For I know that in me (that is, in my flesh)
nothing good dwells;
for to will is present with me,
but how to perform what is good I do not find.
For the good that I will to do, I do not do;
but the evil I will not to do, that I practice.
Now if I do what I will not to do,
it is no longer I who do it,
but sin that dwells in me.[2]

In order to tell a man that it's wrong to steal cars, there must be a moral law system in place that clearly outlines the wrong behavior. If there is no moral law system in place, then how will people know what is right and wrong behavior? How will the man, whose inward nature is to steal cars, know that he shouldn't steal cars? This is the main reason God provides the exhortations and warnings previously mentioned, and others like them.

Love Speech

Love Speech

• CHAPTER 9 •

Spoil Sport,
Or Unbridled Lover
of Your Soul?

ALL MANKIND HAS THE INNATE DESIRE to do whatever pleases them, to do whatever makes them feel good. If we don't like the current system of moral law telling us we shouldn't do this or that, we try to change it in order to be able to do whatever makes us feel good. But' God's law system is not only immutable – unchanging - it is also designed with our best interest in mind. It is designed to show us those behaviors that are wrong and harmful and to point us in the right direction for curing our problem.

Shortly after beginning His ministry, Jesus declared his purpose in coming to Earth:

Love Speech

The Son of Man has come to seek and to save that which was lost."[1]

This begs the question: What was it that God lost? Actually, God wasn't the only one who lost something. Mankind lost something as well. So, what was it that we lost? Well, whatever it was, we lost it all the way back in the Garden of Eden. So, let's go back and take a look at Genesis chapter 3. It turns out that as a result of having been deceived by the enemy, God and all of mankind lost three things.

The first thing we lost was our personal relationship with God. Shortly after Adam and Eve were deceived, God went for a walk through His garden and looked for Adam and Eve to go along with Him, *"Adam, where are you?"*[2] What was Adam and Eve's response? *"Adam and his wife hid themselves from the presence of the LORD God among the trees of the garden. 'I heard Your voice in the garden, and I was afraid because I was naked; and I hid myself.'"*[3] The activities of sin they were involved in caused them to be separated from God – by their own volition!

The second thing we lost was the flow of God's life to us. Remember, God wants you to be a recipient of His love. He wants you to have His success, not failure. His love, not fear. His riches, not poverty. His health, not illness. His life, not death. His joy, not depression. His good things, not bad things. We lost the flow of God's Love and God's life to us.

The third thing we lost was our dominion and rulership responsibilities in His creation. Without a relationship with God, and without His Love and life flowing to us, we were unable to exercise the proper rulership God initially intended us to exercise over His creation:

"Cursed is the ground for your sake; in toil you shall eat of it all the days of your life. Both thorns and thistles it shall bring forth for you, and you shall eat the herb of the field. In the sweat of your face you shall eat bread."[4]

The God-Life that was supposed to flow from God through mankind was to be used to exercise the proper stewardship and care over the rest of God's Creation. However, once man's personal relationship with His Creator was cut off – spiritual death, not just physical death - the flow of that God-Life also ended, and mankind lost his authority and power to tend and steward God's Creation.

The loss of our relationship with God, the loss of the flow of God-Life through us, and the resulting loss of our stewardship over God's Creation were all a direct result of deceitful subterfuge on the part of Satan. The main thrust of the enemy's trickery came in getting Adam and Eve to question the validity of God's Word: *"Has God really said..."*[5]

To call God's directives and warnings which were previously mentioned, and all the others He states in the Bible, "hate speech" is to experience the same deception Adam and Eve suffered under Satan in the Garden of Eden: *Has God really said...*? That is exactly the same tactic of deception mankind's enemy is using today. "Did God really say that homosexuality is an abomination? Is that what He really means?" Isn't that "hate speech?"

Don't be deceived! Yes. That is what God really said. And that is what He really means. It is not hate speech. It is Love Speech! Why would God say that!? Doesn't the Bible say God is Love? Isn't God supposed to love everybody, even the homosexual?

Yes. God is Love.

Yes. God loves all mankind.

But God hates those behaviors and lifestyles that keep us separated from Him and His Love – including homosexuality! *God loves you enough to warn you!* What some men call "love" is not true Love. What some men call "hate speech" is in truth Love Speech!

The problem is not that God is a spoil-sport. The problem is we are selfish by nature. We want to do what *we* want to do. It's like telling a child to quit watching TV and go do homework. What ensues is usually anything from paying no attention whatsoever to the request, to whining, or to belligerent anger. Any of which usually includes accusations of "hate speech." But as any good parent knows it is more important for the child to learn discipline – preferably self-discipline – and get their homework done.

Adults are no different. God also loves you enough to tell you clearly and simply how to restore your relationship with Him, how to restore the flow of His God-Life in you and through you to others, and how to restore your proper position as a steward and ruler in His Kingdom. Children can learn self-discipline… if they chose to do so. Adults can overcome their immoral behavior issues… if they chose to do so. But, both child and adult need someone to help them.

Love Speech

CHAPTER 10

Restoring Ultimate Love!

MOST PEOPLE THINK GOD is mad at them. But He's not. Most people think God is sitting in heaven playing a game something like 'Whack A Mole.' They think God has a big mallet, and every time we break one of His rules, He gets to whack us with that mallet. Most people think their fate depends on their behavior. If they're bad, *Whack!* Go to hell! If they're good, there's no *whack*, and they might get to go to heaven… or, if God is having a bad hair day, they might not. No wonder people mistakenly call the Love Speech of the Bible hate speech. Nothing like this could be further from the truth. God is Love. Love flows from the very essence of His being. You could say Love flows from every pore of His Body.

Love Speech

God is also righteous. Righteousness is another characteristic that flows from the very essence of God's being. God is not responsible for the evil and wickedness and bad things in the world – mankind is responsible. We are the ones who disobeyed God. Evil, wickedness, and death entered the world when Adam and Eve sinned by disobeying God. In God's written Word, His Bible, He warns mankind of the behaviors and lifestyles – what He refers to as sin – that will completely separate us from Him and His Love. Because God is righteous, He will not tolerate nor allow any man or woman who is involved in sinful behaviors to be in His Presence. Because God created us, He expects no less from us.

As with any manmade law, there is a penalty that must be paid when the law is broken. God's righteousness demands that anyone involved in the behaviors He warns us not to participate in – the behaviors He calls sin – must pay a penalty. Breaking God's law demands a penalty to be paid. That penalty is death. Not just physical death, but spiritual death - eternal separation from God.

The wages of sin is death. That is an absolute truth. If you make yourself a slave to any of the sins mentioned previously, or elsewhere in the Bible, you will earn your wages: death. Both physical and spiritual death. But, remember, *"God did not send His Son into the world to condemn the world…"* God did not send Jesus into the world to condemn people to death. He sent Jesus into the world to provide a way for people to avoid death, and to be restored as recipients of His Love. God sent His Son to demonstrate His Love, not to condemn people.

A perfect example of this is when a woman caught in the act of adultery was brought before Jesus.[1] The lawyers of Jesus' day pointed out that under biblical law adultery was a behavior punishable by death. Adultery was - and is - a behavior that separates people from God. For that reason alone, God hates adultery. And those lawyers were correct, under biblical law the penalty for adultery was death by stoning. Two things happened next.

1. Jesus told the woman's accusers that whichever of them was without sin could throw the first stone. All those legalists were ready to condemn this woman to death, right then and there. Until Jesus pointed out to them that under biblical law, all of them were also guilty of the death penalty. One by one all those lawyers, because they were also guilty under the law, lost the desire to condemn that woman and put her to death. This is the first thing

today's religious legalists should remember. Under biblical law, we are all guilty of sin. We all deserve to be condemned to death.

2. Once all the legalists had left the scene, Jesus asked the woman, *"Has no one condemned you?* When the woman answered "No", Jesus replied, *"Neither do I condemn you.* (I repeat: *"God did not send His Son into the world to condemn the world, but that the world through Him might be saved."*) *Go your way and <u>sin no more</u>."*

Jesus did not condemn the woman because of her sin. But – notice carefully! Jesus did not disregard or overlook her sin either. He was not tolerant of her sin. *"Go your way <u>and sin no more</u>!"* Jesus clearly called adultery a sin that carries the penalty of death. But He did not condemn her. He urgently admonished her to stop that kind of harmful behavior! "Don't play with the electrical outlet of adultery! You'll get hurt!" Why did He say that? Because adultery will keep her from having a relationship with God, and it will keep her from God's Love. Ultimately, if she continues a lifestyle of that type of behavior, it will permanently separate her from God for all eternity.

That is Love Speech!

Love Speech

More than the woman's immoral behavior of adultery, Jesus was most concerned about the woman's relationship with God and allowing her the opportunity to restore that relationship! John 3:16 *"God **so loved** the world that He gave His only begotten Son**, that whoever believes in Him should not perish but have everlasting life!"** Those legalistic lawyers were in no way concerned with the relationship that woman could have and should have with God. Their only concern was to trick Jesus by the law so they could kill Him. And if they had to kill the woman to be able to kill Jesus, that was okay with them. Their entire focus was on condemning the woman so they could condemn Jesus. That is hate speech!

It is one thing to warn people that their wrong behavior will lead to death. That is Love Speech. It is another thing entirely to condemn people because of their immoral behavior. That is hate speech.

So... if adultery is a sin punishable by death under biblical law, why did Jesus tell the woman, *"Go your way..."*? Did this mean that Jesus loved the woman so much that He left her free to continue her adulterous behavior and lifestyle so she could do whatever made her feel good? No. He also sternly warned her to *"...sin no more."* Jesus knew He would be paying the penalty for that woman's sin, along with the sins of all of the rest of us. Yet that did not leave her free to pursue her sinful, harmful behavior. Remember: God loves you. God does not condemn people who are involved in wrong behaviors and lifestyles. Yet, neither does God condone or confirm these behaviors and lifestyles just because He loves us. Once we accept the death of Jesus as the payment for the penalty of our sins, God expects us to overcome our immoral behavior and lifestyle.

Love Speech

•   CHAPTER 11   •

Love In Action

There is a part of Love Speech we do not hear often enough. We need to remember, '*The wages of sin is death...*' But there is no period at the end of that sentence. That is *not* the end of the report. Now we get to the heart of God's Love Speech:

> *For the wages of sin is death,*
> **but the free gift of God is eternal life**
> **in Christ Jesus our Lord!**[1]

God is not a spoil-sport eagerly waiting to whack people over the head with a mallet. As we began our look into Love Speech we learned that God is Love. Love is the essence of the nature and character of God. Ever since Adam and Eve were tricked into disobedience by Satan, God has been pursuing mankind with all the Love He has in order to restore our relationship with Him. Since the events of the

69

Garden of Eden, God has been pursuing mankind year after year century after century, millennium after millennium with an endless Love.

But we also learned that God is righteous. Righteousness is the essence of the nature and character of God. And God's righteousness demands that justice be carried out when the penalty for sin is required to be paid. God's predicament is this: how can a righteous God uphold justice without losing forever the object of His Love – mankind?

Mankind is in an equally dire predicament. There is nothing in our character or nature that allows us to meet God's demand for righteousness. It is a problem we are incapable of fixing by ourselves. Thousands of years of effort - or lack of effort - have proven our inability to change ourselves for the better. God provided the only solution to His problem and to ours. That solution requires nothing less than the death of God Himself.

Because God is Love – because His love for us is so overwhelming – He has gone to the most extreme lengths to make a way for us to come into His Presence, to restore our relationship with Him. *The wages of sin is death.* God Himself agreed to pay the penalty for our wrongdoings, He agreed to take our death sentence on Himself and to die in our place.

Now that is Love! That is what Jesus did on the Cross. With the death penalty for our sins paid by Jesus Christ, the way is now open for our relationship with God to be restored. Folks, God is not the one who got mad and left us. We are the ones who left Him! We were disobedient. We broke off the relationship. We left God. But God never gave up on us. He came looking for us in the Garden, and He is still looking for us today, six thousand years later, in order to restore our relationship with Him so He can let His love flow to us. That is Love! Notice that all of this is a "*free gift*" from God. His free gift is available to everyone.

The Lord is… longsuffering toward us, not willing that any should perish but that all should come to change the way they think.[2]

Change the way they think about what? About God's Love Speech. Quit calling it hate speech and hear it for what it really is. The Love-born cry of your Creator asking you to quit doing those behaviors that separate you from Him. All the while He knows that you are incapable of saving yourself. So, He does it all for you.

We now have two options. The choice is yours. Receive God's gift of Love. Or not. We can earn the slave wages of sin. Or, we can receive the free gift of Love. The slave wages of sin are death. The free Love Gift of God is eternal life in Christ Jesus.

The best part of that free gift is this: in no way does it depend on how we behave. Just like the woman caught in adultery, there is nothing we can do – no good work, no penance, no sacrifice - there is nothing we can do to earn this gift. That's what makes it a gift. When a real gift is given there is no way to repay the giver.

CHAPTER 12

Love Speech and the Free Gift

ALL OF GOD'S LOVE SPEECH is designed to show us how valuable we are to Him and the overwhelming power of His love for us.

The main danger we face is when we call God's Love Speech hate speech. This was the original problem Adam and Eve faced. God had instructed them not to eat from the tree of the knowledge of good and evil. Satan's original deception was to get them to question God's Love Speech: *"Did God really say...?* Adam and Eve *"saw that the tree was good for food, that it was pleasant to the eyes, and a tree desirable to make one wise, they took of its fruit and ate."*[1] They believed the hate speech and did what made them "feel good." The end result was death:

Love Speech

Therefore, just as through one man sin entered the world, and death through sin, and thus death spread to all men, because all sinned .[2]

But God loves you too much to let you die. So, He died in your place:

God demonstrates His own love toward us, in that while we were still sinners, Christ died for us.[3]

Who Himself bore our sins in His own body on the tree, that we, having died to sins, might live…"[4]

In order to receive God's free gift of love, we must believe His Love Speech, we must believe what He says in His Word:

As many as received Him, to them He gave the right to become children of God, to those who believe in His name.[5]

Believe on the Lord Jesus Christ, and you will be saved.[6]

Jesus came *"to seek and to save that which was lost."* What was lost was our Love relationship with God, the God-Life that flows through that Love relationship, and our position as reigning stewards in God's Kingdom. God's greatest desire is to restore these through His Son Jesus Christ. God never made it hard for us to come to Him and receive His love. There are really only two things we need to do:[7]

> 1) *If you confess with your mouth the Lord Jesus,*
>
> 2) *and believe in your heart that God has raised Him from the dead, you will be saved.*

To receive God's Love requires us to:

1. Speak God's Love Speech out loud, saying: "Jesus be my Lord."
2. Sincerely believe in our heart that God raised Jesus from the dead… just as He says He did in His Word.

You can pray a prayer as simple as this:

Lord God, it was you who created me, it was you who pursued me relentlessly with all Your Love, it was You who died on the Cross for me, paying the penalty for all my sins.

Lord, I yield my heart, my soul, and my mind to You and to Your Love Speech. I believe with all my heart that You raised Jesus from the dead.

Love Speech

Jesus, I yield to Your Love Speech, bowing my heart before You, and I ask you to be my Lord. Lord, I am a recipient of Your Love right here and right now.

God, Your Love Speech says that by Your power when I receive Jesus as my Lord, I become Your child. Your Love Speech says that in Christ Jesus I have become a new creation. Thank You, Father, my old life is over and my new life in Christ Jesus has begun. Amen.

Awesome! Your relationship with God has just been restored. As you grow in your relationship with the Lord, God's Love and God's life will begin to flow to you. Learning to walk with God day-by-day requires patience and diligence. God is there to help you, step-by-step. There are a few key factors that will help you grow in your new relationship with God:

1. Learn to read and study His Word. Faith comes by hearing God. Hearing comes by God's Word.[8] God speaks to you through His written Word – the Bible. As you read, God will cause different verses to come alive in your heart. (Don't worry, you'll know it when it happens!) This is His way of showing you the lessons you need to learn in order to grow

in your relationship with Him. Don't get impatient. All relationships take time.

2. Learn to pray. Prayer is just talking with God. Ask Him to teach you from His Word. Ask Him questions about His Word. Questions don't bother Him; He appreciates your desire to know Him better. Just remember, prayer is a two-way conversation. You talk and He listens. Then He talks and you listen. Remember, "*hearing comes by the Word of God.*" (An excellent book to get started in your prayer life is *Restoring Order In A Chaotic World*, available at the Ginosko House website.)

3. Begin to develop new friendships and associations with other Christians. Ask God to help you find a good church, one that preaches from the Bible. Go to the meetings consistently and begin to participate. Ask God to help you connect with the believers He wants you to connect with.

Beneficiaries of His Love

As you grow stronger in your walk with the Lord, you will begin to find more of His promises and benefits in His Love Speech. Remember two things:

Love Speech

1. These benefits don't just fall on us like ripe cherries off a tree. Yes, as a loving Father, God looks after us. But we are required to press into our relationship with Him, to get to know Him better and better each day. God-Life is knowing Him, not knowing about Him.[9]

2. God's benefits and promises aren't just for you and you alone. God does good things for you so you can do good things for others. Remember, someone loved you enough to tell you about God's Love Speech, even though you thought it was hate speech!

God's Love for you is unfathomable. What follows is just a shortlist of what He makes available for you through His Love.

The Short List of God's Benefits[10]

Healing & Health

Isaiah 53:5
He was wounded for our transgressions, He was bruised for our iniquities;
the chastisement for our peace was upon Him, and by His stripes we are healed.

1 Peter 2:24-25
Who Himself bore our sins in His own body on the tree, that we, having died to sins, might

Love Speech

*live for righteousness —
by whose stripes you were healed.*
Romans 8:11
*The Spirit of Him who raised Jesus from the
dead dwells in us, and He who raised Christ
from the dead...energizes, quickens, and gives
life to our mortal body through His Spirit who
dwells in us.*

Psalm 107:19-20
*He saved them out of their distresses.
He sent His word and healed them,
and delivered them
from their destructions.*

Jeremiah 33:6
*I will heal them and reveal to them
the abundance of peace and truth.*

Proverbs 4:20-22
*My son, give attention to my words; incline
your ear to my sayings.
Do not let them depart from your eyes; keep
them in the midst of your heart;
for they are life to those who find them, and
health to all their flesh.*

Love Speech

Prosperity

Psalm 35:27-28
Let them shout for joy and be glad,
who favor Your righteous cause;
let them say continually,
'Let the Lord be magnified,
who takes pleasure in the prosperity
of His servant.'

Philippians 4:19
My God supplies all my need according to His
riches in glory in Christ Jesus.

Luke 6:38
Give, and it will be given to you:
good measure, pressed down,
shaken together, and running over
will be put into your bosom.
For with the same measure that you use,
it will be measured back to you."

Proverbs 10:22
The blessing of the Lord makes one rich,
and You add no sorrow with it.

Psalm 23:1
The Lord is my Shepherd, I shall not lack.

Love Speech

God-Life

When the Bible talks about "life" and "eternal life", most of the time it is talking about God-Life, the life that flows from God to all believers through Jesus Christ.

John 17:3-4
This is eternal life,
that they may know You,
the only true God,
and Jesus Christ whom You have sent.

John 6:63-64
It is the Spirit who gives life;
the flesh profits nothing.
The words that I speak to you are spirit
and they are life.

John 5:24
Most assuredly, I say to you,
he who hears My word and believes in Him
who sent Me has everlasting life,
and shall not come into judgment,
but has passed from death into life.

Proverbs 12:28
In the way of righteousness is life,
and in its pathway there is no death.

Love Speech

1 John 5:11-12

And this is the testimony:
that God has given us eternal life,
and this life is in His Son.
He who has the Son has life;
he who does not have the Son of God
does not have life.

1 John 1:1-4

That which was from the beginning,
which we have heard, which we have seen
with our eyes, which we have looked upon,
and our hands have handled, concerning the
Word of life —
the life was manifested, and we have seen,
and bear witness, and declare to you that
eternal life which was with the Father
and was manifested to us —
that which we have seen and heard
we declare to you, that you also may have
fellowship with us;
and truly our fellowship is with the Father
and with His Son Jesus Christ.
And these things we write to you
that your joy may be full.

Love Speech

Wisdom & Understanding

Proverbs 1:7
The fear of the LORD
is the beginning of knowledge,
but fools despise wisdom and instruction.

Proverbs 9:10
The fear of the LORD
is the beginning of wisdom,
and the knowledge of the Holy One
is understanding.

1 Corinthians 1:30
But of Him you are in Christ Jesus,
who became for us wisdom from God.

1 Corinthians 2:16
We have the mind of Christ.

Ephesians 1:15-19
Therefore I also, after I heard of your faith in
the Lord Jesus
and your love for all the saints,
do not cease to give thanks for you,
making mention of you in my prayers:
that the God of our Lord Jesus Christ,
the Father of glory, may give to you the spirit
of wisdom and revelation in the knowledge of
Him, the eyes of your understanding being

Love Speech

*enlightened; that you may know what is the
hope of His calling, what are the riches of the
glory of His inheritance in the saints,
and what is the exceeding greatness of His
power toward us who believe.*

Love: Mercy & Grace

God expresses His Love toward us through His
mercy and grace. God's mercy and grace are:

- His compassion toward us, even when we
  deserve punishment.
- His commitment to restore us, even though
  we deserve to endure the punishment of
  our sin.
- His covenant Love expressed through the
  covenant blood of Jesus Christ at the point
  of our greatest foolishness.

Psalm 103 outlines the benefits of God's mercy
and grace this way:

1. He forgives all our sins.
2. He takes He takes away all our
   unrighteousness and gives us
   Jesus' righteousness.
3. He heals all our diseases.
4. He redeems and separates our life
   from destruction.

5. He crowns us with lovingkindness and tender mercies.
6. He satisfies our mouth with good things.
7. He renews our youth like the eagle's.
8. He executes righteousness and judgment for us against all oppression, He sets us free.
9. He makes known His ways to us.

Sin loses its hold over you

As you grow in your relationship with God, you will find that sin no longer has dominion over you:

Romans 6:14

For sin shall not have dominion over you, for you are not under law but under grace.

God restores your place in His Kingdom

God will also begin to restore your rulership in His Kingdom:

Romans 5:17

For if by the one man's offense death reigned through the one, much more those who receive abundance of grace and of the gift of righteousness will reign in life through the One, Jesus Christ.

Love Speech

You grow to become an imager of Christ

As you grow in your relationship with God, you begin to take on the image and nature of Christ:

2 Corinthians 3:18

We all, with unveiled face,
beholding as in a mirror the glory of the Lord,
are being transformed into the same image
from glory to glory,
just as by the Spirit of the Lord.

Taking on the image of Christ includes taking on the following characteristics:

2 Cor. 5:17	A new creation.
2 Cor. 5:21	Righteousness of God in Christ.
Prov. 28:1	Bold as a lion.
Eph. 1:4	Holy and without blame.
Rom. 8:37	More than a conqueror.
Eph. 1:6	Accepted of God.
Eph. 2:10	God's workmanship.
Col. 2:9-10	Complete in Him.
Rom. 8:17	Joint-heir with Christ.
Rev. 1:6; 5:6	King and priest unto God.
1 Jn 4:4; 5:4-5	An overcomer.
2 Cor. 5:20	An ambassador of Christ.

Love Speech

However, the greatest characteristic of God you will begin to take on is His Love. Love is the very essence of the nature and character of God, and as you take on the image of Christ, Love will grow to become your character and nature as well. What is the nature and character of Love? It's how God pursued you with all of His Love when you were hurling accusations of "hate speech":

Love suffers long and is kind;
love does not envy;
love does not parade itself,
love is not puffed up;
love does not behave rudely,
love does not seek its own,
love is not provoked,
love keeps no account of evil;
love does not rejoice in iniquity,
but rejoices in the Truth;
love bears all things, believes all things,
hopes all things, endures all things.
Love never fails.[11]

These are but a handful of the benefits and promises of God. The key in all of this is relationship. John 17:3 clearly states that eternal life, the God-kind of Life, is knowing God through personal experience. It is far more than just knowing about God. These benefits and promises come through a close personal relationship with the God who Loves you!

And don't worry. If you quit the relationship, He will always be waiting for you to return to Him. And if you mess up and disobey - we all do from time-to-time - God has given you a "bar of soap" to clean up with:

If we confess our sins, He is faithful
and just to forgive us our sins
and to cleanse us from
all unrighteousness.[12]

Be honest and open with Him about your mistakes. We have all just begun a new way of life and a new relationship with the God who created us and Loves us. He will clean you right up and keep right on Loving you. But always remember, the biggest benefit of all is this:

Nothing can ever again
separate *you* from God's Love!

Yet in all these things we are more than
conquerors through Him who loved us.
For I am persuaded that neither death nor
life, nor angels nor principalities nor powers,
nor things present nor things to come, nor
height nor depth, nor any other created thing,

Love Speech

*shall be able to separate us
from the love of God which is in
Christ Jesus our Lord!*[13]

Love Speech

Endnotes

Chapter 1

1. <https://www.dictionary.com/browse/hate-speech>

2.< https://sonsoflibertymedia.com/anti-theist-penn-jillette-much-hate-somebody-believe-everlasting-life-possible-not-tell/>

3. Ibid.

Chapter 2

1. Underhill, Evelyn, *"If God were small enough to be understood, He would not be big enough to be worshipped."* (Your problem is, you're not big enough, powerful enough, or smart enough to be God.)

2. Deuteronomy 12:8; Jud. 17:6

2. Isaiah 5:21

3. Proverbs 30:13

4. Proverbs 12:15

Chapter 3

1. John 17:17

Chapter 4

1. Loeffler, John & Carol, *Critical Thinking in an Age of Deceit*, DVD

Chapter 5
1. 1 John 4:8, 16
2. Psalm 5:4
3. Isaiah 59:2
4. John 17:3

Chapter 6
1. Leviticus 19:17-18

Chapter 7
1. Deuteronomy 5:3
2. Deuteronomy 5: 4-6
3. Missler, Chuck, *The Invisible War: Against The Gods of Egypt*, Personal News Update Journal, Koinonia House, Jul. 2000. <https://www.khouse.org/articles/2000/263/print/>
4. Deuteronomy 5:7
5. Deuteronomy 5:8-11
6. Deuteronomy 5:12
7. Deuteronomy 5:13
8. Deuteronomy 5:14
9. Deuteronomy 5:15
10. Deuteronomy 5:16
11. Deuteronomy 5:17
12. Ecclesiastes 12:11

Love Speech

Chapter 8
1. Tremblay, Richard, et. al., *Physical Aggression During Early Childhood: Trajectories and Predictors,* <https://www.ncbi.nlm.nih.gov/pmc/articles/PMC3283570/>
2. Romans 7:18-20

Chapter 9
1. Luke 19:10
2. Genesis 3:9
3. Genesis 3:10
4. Genesis 3:17-19
5. Genesis 3:1

Chapter 10
1. John 8:2-12

Chapter 11
1. Romans 6:23
2. 2 Peter 3:9

Chapter 12
1. Genesis 3:6
2. Romans 5:12
3. Romans 5:8
4. 1 Peter 2:24
5. John 1:12
6. Acts 16:31

Love Speech

7. Romans 10:9
8. Romans 10:17
9. John 17:3
10. Psalm 68:19
11. 1 Corinthians 13:4-14:1
12. 1 John 1:9
13. Romans 8:37-39

Love Speech